Sports World

Skiing

Donna Bailey

STECK-VAUGHN
LIBRARY
A Division of Steck-Vaughn Company

We're going on a ski trip.
First, I learn to ski at the dry ski center.

2

I put on my boots and go outside.
Our teacher tells us how to
put on our skis.

My hard boots and long skis feel funny.
Our teacher makes us lift up each leg
to get used to the feel of the skis.

4

Then he shows us how to side step
up the slope so the metal edges
of our skis grip the matting.

My teacher shows me how to make a
V-shape with my skis to stop sliding downhill.
This is called a snowplow.

6

It's my turn to go down the slope.
I keep my skis straight and get to
the bottom without falling down.

After lots of practice, I can even ski
down the slope with my arms in the air!

After a few more lessons, my teacher
says I can try the big slope.
I ride up to the top on the ski lift.

It seems a long way down, but I remember
to snowplow when I want to slow down.

Soon it's time for our trip.
There's lots of snow at the ski resort.
The sun is very bright, so I wear
dark glasses.

I stand at the top of the easiest slope.
The snow feels very slippery.

I start sliding down the slope, so
I try a snowplow to slow down.

I lose my balance and fall down.
The snow is much softer to fall on
than the matting on the dry ski slope.

It isn't easy to get up.
I put my skis together across the slope
and push myself up with my poles.

Once I'm up, I ski down the slope.

I'm glad I took lessons.

This is fun!

We go skiing every day.
I learn to bend my knees and
to turn without falling over.
I can go faster now.
I ski down the steeper slopes.

Many people enjoy downhill skiing.
Downhill skiers go down a mountain
on special trails called ski runs.

18

This man goes out every morning in
his machine to smooth down
the snow on each run.

Different kinds of lifts take people
to the top of each run.
This is a drag lift that pulls from behind.

Drag lifts take people up slopes
that are not very steep.

Chair lifts take people to steeper runs high on the mountain.

Pole markers along the side make it easy for skiers to stay on the run.

Skiers who want to go to the steepest runs
at the top of the mountain can ride
in a gondola car.

These runs are for expert skiers.
They ski very fast!

Good downhill skiers can travel
50 miles an hour
down the mountain.

Ski jumping is fun, too, but
it takes a lot of practice.

Some skiers can jump a long way.

Ski jumpers at the Winter Olympics
look as if they are flying.

Some people like to ski on
a single board called a monoski.
They use their bodies to balance and turn.

This man likes cross-country skiing.
His skis are long and narrow with
patterns on the bottom that grip the snow.

Cross-country skiers travel long distances across the mountains, sometimes where there are no trails.

Index

balance, 14, 30

boots 3, 4

chair lift 22

cross-country skiing 31,
  32

downhill skiing 18, 26

drag lift 20, 21

dry ski center 2, 14

glasses 11

gondola car 24

knees 17

lessons 9, 16

monoski 30

mountains 18, 26, 32

Olympics 29

pole markers 23

poles 15

ski jumping 27–29

ski lifts 9, 20

ski resort 11

ski runs 18–22, 24, 25

skis 3–7, 31

snow 11, 12, 14

snow plow 6, 10, 13

Reading Consultant: Diana Bentley
Editorial Consultant: Donna Bailey
Executive Editor: Elizabeth Strauss
Project Editor: Becky Ward

Picture research by Jennifer Garratt
Designed by Richard Garratt Design

Photographs
Cover: Tony Stone Worldwide (Andrew Hourmont)
Allsport: (Gerard Vandystadt)
Peter Greenland: title page,2,3,4,5,6,7,8,9,10,11,12,13,14,15,16, 17,18,19,20,21,22,23,25,27,31,32
Sporting Pictures: 24
Tony Stone Worldwide; 28 (Mark Shapiro), 30 (Jean -Francois Causse), 26

Library of Congress Cataloging-in-Publication Data: Bailey, Donna.   Skiing / Donna Bailey.   p.   cm.—(Sports world) Includes index. SUMMARY: An introduction, in simple text and photographs, to the techniques and equipment of skiing.   ISBN 0-8114-2856-7   1. Skis and skiing—Juvenile literature.   [1. Skis and skiing.]   I. Title. II. Series: Bailey, Donna. Sports world.   GV854.B335 1990   796.93—dc20   90-36125   CIP   AC

ISBN 0-8114-2856-7
Copyright 1991 National Education Corporation
Original copyright Heinemann Children's Reference 1991
1 2 3 4 5 6 7 8 9 0 LB 96 95 94 93 92 91